Strengthening your immune system.
How to fight infection, allergy and autoimmune disease

Dr. Paul Clayton

English UK,

Oxford, UNITED KINGDOM
www.drpaulclayton.eu

ISBN: 978-1-913539-17-7

Editor: Ugnė Naujokaitytė

Introduction

Right up until the early 20th century, infectious diseases were always the most important cause of illness and death. Improved sanitation, vaccination and then antibiotics briefly tipped the scales in our favour but in the 21st century, the infectious diseases are making a comeback. Antibiotic and anti-fungal drugs are losing so much of their effectiveness that if current trends continue, many elements of modern medicine, from anticancer drugs to intensive surgeries, will become unusable. And new viruses, like COVID19 (formerly known as Wuhan virus), are entering the human population at an increasing rate.

Fortunately, we have powerful immune systems that have an amazing ability to keep the bugs at bay. Unfortunately, modern lifestyles have harmed those immune systems. They have not only become less able to protect us, they are increasingly turning against us. We see this in the growing epidemics of allergy and autoimmune disease, and our increased vulnerability to infection.

This book shows how to undo the damage. It contains a set of simple, science-based steps you can use to rebuild your immune system, strengthen your defences and live a healthier life.

Contents

1. The multi-layered immune system: defence in depth

The immune system monitors and defends your body 24 hours a day, every day of your life. It protects against invasion by pathogenic bacteria, viruses, parasites and fungi and, on the relatively few occasions that these gain entry to the body, it fights the resulting infection. It is also one of the body's defences against cancer, and plays a vital role in the recovery from physical injury. A weakened immune system, therefore, leaves you vulnerable to disease.

Many things can weaken the immune system including stress, a poor diet, lack of sleep and long-haul flights. Certain medications such as the steroids and most anti-cancer drugs degrade the immune system, as does excessive consumption of tobacco and alcohol. The Human Immunodeficiency Virus (HIV) is another cause of immune dysfunction.

The immune system is also depleted in the winter months due to falling vitamin D levels, just when adverse weather conditions keep many indoors and in closer contact with others. This combination of factors makes us more likely to give – and get – colds and flu.

The dangers of inadequate or disturbed immune function are very real. In the US and in the UK, more people die each year from systemic bacterial infections than from breast, colorectal and pancreatic cancer combined. And both autoimmune diseases and allergies continue to increase.

Nor can we continue to rely on antibiotics. The rise of 'superbugs', antimicrobial-resistant pathogens such as MRSA, VRSA, the CRE's and TDR-TB (see glossary), shows that the antibiotics are losing their effectiveness. Anti-fungal drugs are beginning to run out of road too, as evidenced by the recent and lethal spread of drug-resistant Candida auris.

Your <u>two</u> immune systems

We talk of an immune system, but in fact **you have two distinct, interconnected immune sub-systems.** These are the innate immune system and the adaptive (or acquired) immune system.

The **adaptive immune system** is that part of the immune system with memory. It is involved positively in immunisation, and negatively in allergy and autoimmunity. Its key cells are lymphocytes, which are sub-divided into T-cells and B-cells.

Once the adaptive immune system has learned to recognize an enemy after an initial infection, and to a lesser extent after vaccination, it remembers the enemy's characteristics. On second exposure to the threat the memory cells recognize it and generate an immune response involving highly specific weapons such as antibodies. That's why it is very unusual to catch measles twice.

The adaptive immune system is powerful, sophisticated and highly specific, but it is initially slow to respond and often insufficient to protect the host against the first onslaught of a virulent bacterium or virus. It is only able to respond rapidly and at peak effectiveness if you have already encountered the threat previously. And its very specificity can be a weakness. After an initial infection, small mutations in a virus or bacterium may be enough to bypass the adaptive immune system. This is why the adaptive immune system is our second line of defence.

Our first line of defence, the **innate immune system**, is constructed quite differently. In evolutionary terms it is much older than the more sophisticated adaptive immune system. It is less specific; it can only recognize a limited number of compounds – around a dozen or so – that commonly occur on the surface of bacteria and yeasts. Its key cellular components are macrophages, neutrophils and natural killer (NK) cells.

Most of these 'front line defensive troops' are constantly patrolling the body, looking out for anything that doesn't belong there. If macrophages spot a bacterium they swallow it and try to digest it. If NK cells recognize a virally infected cell they will kill it to prevent further viral replication, and if they encounter a cancer cell (and recognise it as cancerous) they will kill it to prevent tumour growth and spread.

This makes the innate immune system very important indeed. Insects and other invertebrates – in other words, the majority of animal species – rely solely on an innate immune system. They have no adaptive immune system, and manage very well without one. Another sign of the importance of the innate immune system is that while people born with major defects in their adaptive immune system may live into their 30's, mutations that delete components of the innate immune system invariably cause death in utero.

As the numbers of antibiotic-resistant bacteria in our environment increase, economic and political stresses worsen and flu and other pandemics become more likely (see later), it makes good sense to ensure that your innate immune system is working as effectively as possible.

I described it as less specific, but it is actually an extremely complex system with 6 major functional sub-systems.

The Innate Immune System: 7 sub-systems

1. Physical barriers to infection such as skin, and the acid bath of the stomach.
2. Structural systems that displace microbes. These include the shedding of skin cells, the way saliva washes the teeth, the mucous that lines the respiratory tract to catch inhaled microbes and the ciliated cells that bring that mucous up to the throat, from where it passes to the stomach.
3. Immune cells including macrophages, neutrophils and natural killer cells. These are active in all tissues.
4. Antimicrobial peptides and proteins.
5. Soluble factors such as complement, hydrogen peroxide and hypochlorous acid.
6. Immune enzymes such as lactoperoxidase (LPO), which has the ability to kill many pathogens. LPO protects the eyes, ears, nose and throat, the respiratory, gastrointestinal and genito-urinary tracts, and the mammary glands. It works very closely with the immune cells listed above.
7. The microbiome. If optimally configured, this helps to protect the gastrointestinal tract, and probably other sites as well.

Item 1 is relatively constant in most individuals, although the acid bath of the stomach is disabled by proton pump inhibitor drugs such as cimetidine (Tagamet). The importance of the innate immune system is underlined by the fact that although these drugs provide temporary relief from dyspepsia, they significantly increase the risk of death (1).

Item 2. Some microbial displacement systems can be enhanced by specific nutrients such as the funorans and fucoidans, derived from edible seaweeds (see Chapter 4d).

Items 3 – 7 are greatly affected by diet. There is compelling evidence that they have been degraded by dietary changes which have occurred since circa 1950, and that this has hugely increased our risk of disease and early death (2 -9). There is also extensive evidence that they can be repaired, via simple dietary strategies which are outlined in the following sections.

If you are in good health, these strategies will help to ensure that you remain so. If you are not, they will help you to get well.

2. Why our immune systems are less effective than they used to be

Despite, and indeed partly because of modern healthcare, our immune systems are almost certainly weaker than those of our recent ancestors (ie 3). There are two main reasons for this. Firstly, our environment is too clean; and secondly, our diet is too depleted.

A. Excessive hygiene

Humans evolved in a dirty environment. We have been on the planet for hundreds of thousands of years but soap, antiseptics, disinfectants, canned and frozen foods have only been with us for a few generations, and antibiotics arrived less than a century ago.

During most of our time on this planet our environment was replete with bacterial and viral hazards, and our immune systems were constantly challenged. As we had by necessity evolved with strong immune systems, which mostly worked very well, we survived and multiplied.

Indeed, recent studies have shown that the innate immune system adapts to facing constant challenges and responds to these by up-regulating its state of readiness and effectiveness. The innate immune system learned in particular to recognize molecules called 1-3, 1-6 beta glucans, which occur in the cell walls of moulds and yeasts. These compounds 'prime' innate immune cells such as macrophages and neutrophils, which respond by mounting a strong counter-attack and by becoming generally more effective (10).

In an age before fungicides were routinely sprayed onto every food crop, almost everything we ate was contaminated with yeasts and moulds. This was, paradoxically, one of the main factors that kept our innate immune systems at peak capacity.

In today's over-sanitised environment our immune systems have little exposure to these compounds, leaving our defences less active and less able to neutralise new and unexpected threats. This is one reason why, when we travel to parts of the world where sanitation standards are lower, we routinely fall victim to pathogens that locals have no problems with. Another contributory factor is the modern microbiome, which is damaged by our industrial diet. Our vulnerability to 'Montezuma's revenge' and suchlike is largely due to our damaged innate immune systems.

> *The absence of challenge in today's hygiene-obsessed world has also left our immune systems off-balance, and more prone to react to normally harmless substances such as pollen.*

This has contributed to the on-going epidemics of asthma and allergy, and may also have made autoimmune disease more likely. Allergic and autoimmune conditions are made worse by the modern diet, which is depleted and highly pro-inflammatory.

The weakening of the innate immune system is also implicated in the huge increase in cancer that has occurred in the last half century. Another reason for this increase in cancer is the growing problem of dysnutrition.

B. Modern (Type B) malnutrition

Health researchers increasingly refer to a condition known as dysnutrition, or 'Type B' malnutrition. This is not the sort of malnutrition associated with starving people in the developing countries. Instead it is found in people in industrialised societies who have adequate calories (often more than adequate), but inadequate intakes of vitamins, minerals and phytonutrients. This causes metabolic starvation and chronic inflammation, interlocking problems which cause progressive tissue damage and in this way increase the risk of acquiring the symptoms of a chronic degenerative disease. Type B malnutrition impairs the immune system also, increasing the risk of infectious diseases. In fact, dysnutrition has become the leading cause of early (or preventable) death world-wide (4).

In the population at large, for example, the average person has intakes of vitamin D and selenium that are only about half of the RDA (Recommended Daily Amount). These are just two of the many micronutrients critical to the proper functioning of the immune system. Moreover, the RDA was not established to give an optimum level of nutritional intake, but only enough to prevent deficiency symptoms. The optimum levels of a number of micronutrients are higher than the RDA's. This means that most people have an intake of key micronutrients below the levels needed for optimum immune system function.

It may seem counter-intuitive, but one reason so many of us are depleted in so many micronutrients is that we do not eat enough. Throughout our long history we were much more physically active than we are today. Modern metropolitan folk require only 2000 calories / day, thanks to labour-saving technologies such as the car and the computer. But these are very new technologies. As recently as the 19th century, when most activities involved manual labour, people ate almost twice as much as we do now (5). Due to their high levels of physical activity, however, overweight and obesity were rare. At the same time their high intakes of food – organic, of course, and hardly any of it processed – ensured high intakes of micro- and phytonutrients.

> *The amount of food we eat today has almost halved, and with less food come lower intakes of micro- and phytonutrients. To make matters worse, the foods we eat have declined greatly in quality. We eat less fruit, vegetables, pulses, oily fish, whole grains and fibre than our great-grand-parents did.*

At the same time we consume more refined carbohydrates, fast foods and ultra-processed foods – which contain lots of calories but generally have a low to zero nutrient content (6). We consume ever-increasing amounts of industrial, ultra-processed foods, manufactured by a small number of grossly irresponsible multinational food companies whose toxic products now kill more of us than do the tobacco companies (7-9).

Recent studies of hospital patients found that a staggering 60% were malnourished on admission (11). In 30 to 40% of patients, the malnutrition was sufficiently severe to cause lymphopenia (12, 13), a condition in which numbers of white blood cells are significantly sub-normal. This indicates substantial immuno-suppression and a significantly increased risk of acquiring an infection while in hospital – or anywhere else, for that matter (14).

This is one reason why infection control in hospitals is so difficult. Immuno-compromised patients are being brought into an environment full of antibiotic-resistant bacteria. It is like introducing petrol to flames.

Our defences are weakening, and at the worst possible time.

3. The threats we face

A. Antibiotic misuse and the rise of the 'Super Bugs'

Too many visits to the doctor end with a prescription for an antibiotic. That may be perfectly valid for a severe bacterial infection, but not for coughs and colds. These are usually caused by viruses, which cannot be treated with antibiotics. Nevertheless, nearly half of children with common colds are treated with antibiotics (15). Because children catch an average of three to eight colds each year, they may be given many courses of unnecessary antibiotics.

> *In fact, children with colds, ear infections, sinus infections, bronchitis and sore throats account for a staggering three quarters of all antibiotic prescriptions.*

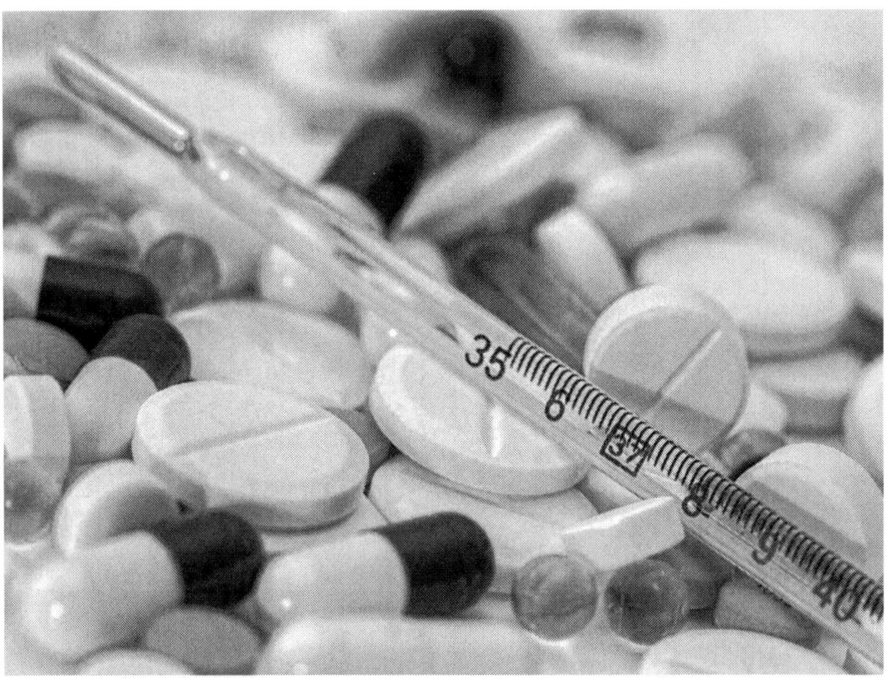

Although doctors know that antibiotics are inappropriate in such cases, they often find themselves pressured to prescribe them to show demanding parents that something – anything – is being done (16).

This is just one instance of inappropriate use of antibiotics, a potentially dangerous and ultimately self-defeating activity because antibiotic overuse inevitably leads to antibiotic resistance. This is an example of natural selection in action.

Bacteria breed faster than we do

Bacteria have a shorter life cycle than ours, and DNA that is somewhat less stable, so they continually and rapidly produce genetic variants.

Take the case of a patient with a thriving bacterial infection. Impose an antibiotic on this unruly mass of micro-organisms and if the right antibiotic was chosen, the vast majority of the bacteria die. Only a few bacteria

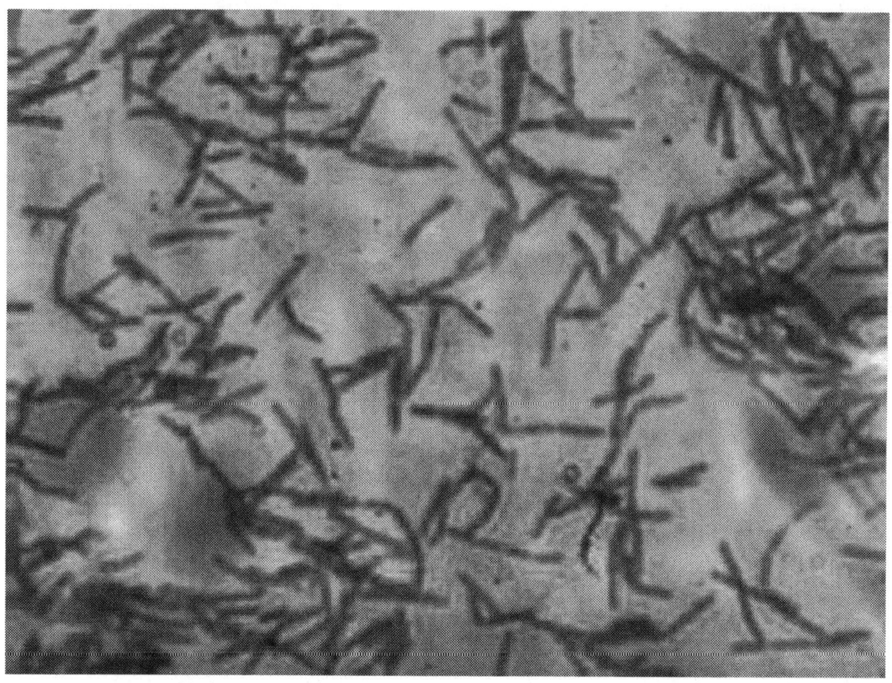

linger on, and if the patient's immune system is working properly it will finish them off.

However, if the antibiotic is given at too low a dose, or too infrequently, or the course is not completed, those bacteria which were slightly more resistant to the antibiotic survive in larger numbers. Among their descendants, those with the strongest resistance survive preferentially; and within a surprisingly short period of time, full-blown resistance can emerge.

Increasingly, however, the primary infection is caused by the drug-resistant strains now prevalent in the community, and even more so in the hospitals. The rising tide of 'superbugs' is a warning of bad times to come. People are becoming increasingly nervous about going to hospital for any kind of treatment, and if current trends continue many surgical procedures, and immnosuppressive drugs such as those used to treat cancer, will become too hazardous to use.

Leading bacteriologists tell us that the world is running out of effective antibiotics. The situation is worsened by the fact that many drug companies abandoned antibiotic research in the 1990's as being too difficult, and insufficiently profitable (17).

"We see a relentless increase in antibiotic resistance across all classes of drug."

Prof. George Poste,
Director of the Biodesign Institute at Arizona State University, 2010

"We are facing a post-antibiotic apocalypse."

Professor Sally Davies, Chief Medical Officer, UK, 2019.

B. Modern lifestyles ...

Stress

Stress management is essential for a healthy immune system. In stressful situations, our adrenal glands secrete the hormone cortisol. Acute stress can be highly productive, but when cortisol output is high and sustained, as it is with chronic stress, the immune system is suppressed.

Most surveys show that significant numbers of people now report feeling stressed on a regular basis. Stress can come from many sources such as work place pressure, the frustration of long commuting times, family concerns and economic insecurity. All these stressors can damage immune function and are undoubtedly increasing, due to a generation of destructive and corrupt politicians whose desire to enrich themselves far exceeds their willingness to enhance the lives of the people they supposedly represent.

A stress-relieving activity of some sort is strongly recommended. There are many to choose from ranging from meditation, to gardening, to voting the bums out of office and blowing up the houses of parliament. (This is an ancient and much-loved British tradition.)

Mass transport

Millions of us have to commute on mass transport systems that are both stressful and over-crowded, creating ideal conditions for the transmission of bacteria and viruses.

If we fly long-haul, exposure to higher levels of ionising radiation temporarily weakens our immune systems, which also contributes to an increased risk of infections. A trans-Atlantic flight exposes you to the same amount of radiation as 2 chest x-rays.

Moreover, rapid global travel means that on any given day, passengers are smuggling infectious agents around the globe.

Which leads us to the pending flu pandemic.

C. The flu, and emergent viruses

The experts say, unanimously, that a flu pandemic will occur. In 2004 the W.H.O. issued a stark warning:

> *"There will be another major pandemic. In the best case we expect billions to fall ill, with 2 to 7 million deaths – but it could be far worse."*

Klaus Stohr, WHO Global Influenza Program

Stohr and his colleagues are convinced there will be a pandemic because history shows that flu pandemics occur every 30 years or so. After this time the genetic makeup of a flu virus has changed so much that any immunity built up from previous exposure no longer applies; while the numbers of children and young adults without prior exposure (and no immunological memory) have also increased (18).

There were three pandemics in the 20th century, all of which spread worldwide within a year of being detected. In 1918 – 1919 the Spanish flu (which actually originated in Northern France) killed around 50 million people. In 1957 the Asian flu pandemic killed a million, and in 1968 Hong Kong flu killed another million or so. In 1997 and subsequently, Bird flu killed a few hundred and in 2009 Swine flu killed an estimated 18.000.

We know that more pandemics are coming. Depending on how the genetic dice roll it the next one could be as minor as the Bird flu, or it could be as serious as the Spanish flu. We have a good idea where it might start; the virus often originates in pigs or poultry, so virologists keep a close eye on environments where large numbers of humans and livestock live close together, such as in parts of China. The virus which may have come from Wuhan (Covid-19), is currently causing a good deal of concern. This coronavirus does not appear to be Disease X, which is still in our future.

> *Antibiotics are ineffective in treating viral infections.*

The right vaccines to protect us against the new strain of flu will take up to 6 months to produce in large amounts, which will be too late for many. Antiviral drugs such as Tamiflu are not particularly effective, and in any case will only be available to a fraction of the population. And it didn't take long for Tamiflu resistance to emerge .. (19).

But it isn't just new flu strains we need to be aware of. Other viruses are appearing in the human population, many for the first time, and at increasing rates. These so-called emergent viruses typically originate in animal species (as the flu virus does) and at some point jump into the human community. Chikungunya, Crimean-Congo haemorrhagic fever, dengue, Ebola, Japanese encephalitis, Kyasanur forest disease, Marburg, MERSA, Nipah, SARS, Wuhan, Zika and others are appearing more and more frequently, as human populations increase and come into contact with new animal species and habitats.

Modern air travel makes it possible to acquire an exciting new virus on one continent and arrive with it in another before the first symptoms of infection emerge; making control extremely difficult. This was the basis for the 2011 film Contagion, which portrayed an extreme but plausible world pandemic.

Summary

The above analysis is not intended to alarm but to make the case for investing in a strong immune status, for you and those you care for.

> *Best practice should include a diet rich in fruits, vegetables, oily fish and wholegrain foods. It should include adequate sleep, reasonable amounts of exercise, and stress reduction where appropriate.*

It should include a well-designed nutritional supplement to provide the baseline wide-spectrum support required for optimum immune health. And it should also include those key nutrients which enhance the innate immune system. These include the 1-3, 1-6 beta glucans, blended prebiotics, and the very specific micro- and phytonutrients required by the immune enzyme lactoperoxidse. Factor in a long and asymptomatic incubation period, and you have an uncontainable global problem - as is happening today with Covid-19.

4. Natural immuno-enhancers

A. 1-3, 1-6 beta glucans

Of all the natural compounds known to activate or prime the innate immune system, the best documented and most effective are the 1-3, 1-6 beta glucans, derived from baker's yeast (20-25). When the US Department of Defence evaluated over 300 potential immuno-enhancers, 1-3, 1-6 beta glucans from yeast had the highest score of all.

The 1-3, 1-6 beta glucans are complex molecules which occur in the cell walls of fungi and yeasts. The innate immune system long ago developed the ability to recognize 1-3, 1-6 beta glucans and react to them by mounting an immune response. But it went further than that. As yeasts are so universal, the innate immune system became dependent on them to function at peak effectiveness.

Then, very late in evolutionary terms, modern technology effectively sterilised our food chain and much of our environment. Levels of yeast and fungi in our foods and in our immediate environment dropped away, and the lack of 1-3, 1-6 beta glucan left the innate immune system weaker and imbalanced.

> *Adding 1-3, 1-6 beta glucans back into the diet primes the innate immune system and restores its normal function and effectiveness.*

For an illustrated explanation of how the 1-3, 1-6 beta glucans work, see Appendix A.

The evidence

- Reduced Infection:

The ability of 1-3, 1-6 beta glucans to activate macrophages and prime neutrophils has been extensively tested in over 800 studies (26-31); and has been shown to protect animals against otherwise fatal infections (32-40).

In one trial, 90% of laboratory animals exposed to very high levels of E-coli survived when their innate immune systems were primed by 1-3, 1-6 beta glucans as opposed to 0% survival in the control group. In a parallel study, 80% survived exposure to high levels of Staphylococcus aureus as opposed to 0% in the control group (41).

When beta glucans were administered in combination with antibiotics after exposure to bacteria, the number of bacteria needed to actually create infection was increased by up to 2,000-fold (42, 43). These tests showed hugely significant improvements in immune function which were duplicated in later, even more dramatic studies. Scientists at the Canadian Department of Defence gave mice 1-3,1-6 beta glucan for seven days before exposing them to a lethal dose of anthrax. Half of the control mice died, but the entire beta glucan-treated group survived (44).

Studies on influenza show a similar pattern. Mice were given beta glucan for seven days before being exposed to flu virus. This particularly virulent strain of virus killed all of the control animals but remarkably, over half of the beta glucan-treated animals survived (45).

Even more persuasively, beta glucan protects pigs. The yeast extract reduces the harm done to the lungs after infection with swine flu virus, and the enhanced immune system is then better able to reduce replication of the virus (46). As pigs and people have a good deal in common (metabolically and physiologically speaking), the pig model is very relevant to our own situation.

There are also a number of clinical trials where beta glucan has been shown to reduce the risk of post-operative sepsis, and which are very much in line with the animal findings (47-50).

- Reduced Radiation damage

1-3, 1-6 beta glucan stimulates the regeneration of white blood cells after bone marrow suppression caused by radiation. This occurs in cancer patients undergoing radiation therapy. Less obviously it also happens in air travellers who are relatively unprotected by atmospheric shielding and are therefore exposed to increased levels of cosmic radiation.

Laboratory studies show that when 1-3, 1-6 beta glucan is given together with a lethal dose of radiation, over 50% of mice survive in contrast to 100% mortality amongst mice who are not given beta glucans (51). In clinical medicine, radiation-related deaths are largely due to the fact that radiation reduces white blood cell count and leaves the patient vulnerable to infection. In the animal studies, the protective effects of the beta glucan were mediated by an accelerated restoration of white blood cell counts; a finding now being explored by cancer specialists, as it makes radiotherapy safer.

The US army took careful note of these results. Starting in the late '80's, the Armed Forces Radiobiology Research Institute ran an exhaustive test program to measure the immuno-protective effects of beta glucan and other immuno-primers, and as recently as 2004 reported that 1-3, 1-6 beta glucan was the most effective of them all. Not only did it protect against infection with bacteria, viruses and fungi, it also conferred protection against radiation injury (52, 53).

For most of us, however, stress, daily travel, super bugs, winter colds and the ongoing COVID-19 pandemic are greater causes for concern; and in any case, the beta glucans are too good to be left to the armed forces. As the age of antibiotics wanes and the threats advance, it makes good sense to include a yeast-derived 1-3, 1-6 beta glucan in your nutritional regime. If you're still not convinced, there is evidence that these compounds may also slow ageing of the immune system (54).

- Safety

Beta glucans have always been in our environment and in our food, and are non-toxic (55, 56). This was accepted by the FDA, which designates 1-3, 1-6 beta glucan as GRAS (Generally Recognised As Safe); and by the European regulatory authorities, who have permitted the sale of beta glucan-enriched soup and beer in Germany.

> *Yeast-derived beta glucan is safe for adults, children and infants, and is now included in infant formulae where the beta glucans mimic some of the immuno-enhancing effects of breast milk (57).*

Some nutritional therapists believe that continuous use of 1-3, 1-6 beta glucans is potentially harmful, but this is based on a fundamental misunderstanding of these compounds' mode of action. Our innate immune systems are designed to cope with constant priming, and depend on it to function properly. More formally, the idea that chronic immuno-priming could be harmful was squashed by a report which showed that life-long exposure to immuno-primers actually extended life (58). Additional work in progress shows that the 1-3, 1-6 beta glucans should probably be classified as essential micronutrients (59).

- Allergy

Pure beta glucan does not trigger allergic or autoimmune symptoms because it has no adverse effect on the adaptive (or acquired) immune system, which is centrally involved in those problems (60). Indeed, by tricking the adaptive immune system into 'thinking' that there is an ongoing infection, the adaptive immune system changes in a way which makes it less likely to develop allergy symptoms (61, 62).

- Transplant

patients should only use 1-3, 1-6 beta glucan carefully and under medical guidance. As beta glucan improves many aspects of immune function, it could theoretically increase the risk of graft rejection. This has not been documented, but caution is still advisable. Nor have adverse effects been seen in patients with autoimmune disease.

- Alternative Sources

1-3, 1-6 beta glucan compounds occur in several plants with a history of medicinal use such as aloe vera and Echinacea, and in medicinal mushrooms such as Shitake and Maitake. These beta glucan compounds have a different structure to the beta glucan in yeast; but whereas the critical CR3 receptor (see Appendix A) fits yeast-derived beta glucan exactly, it does not recognise plant or mushroom derivates as easily. This makes sense. Our immune systems needed to develop a defence against yeast infections. We are rarely invaded by mushrooms.

That is why mushroom and plant derivates are not as good or as consistent immuno-primers as the beta glucan derived from brewer's yeast (63). An animal study at the James Brown Cancer Centre showed Echinacea to have only a very minor effect on immune function when combined with monoclonal antibody cancer therapy. The 100-day survival rate was 10% with Echinacea, but over 90% with yeast-derived 1-3, 1-6 beta glucans.

- Who needs Beta Glucans?

A beta glucan supplement can be taken as a daily supplement in periods of extra stress or threat. This applies to people who are at immediate risk of infection, taking immuno-suppressant medication or experiencing slow and incomplete healing. Long-haul air travellers and those about to enter hospital, for example for elective surgery, are also prime candidates. Many take a beta glucan supplement at the first sign of a cold or sore throat, and during the main winter months. This is especially important for people regularly travelling or working in crowded environments.

1-3, 1-6 beta glucan should be taken daily as the life span of neutrophils, the key effector cells of the innate immune system, is 3 days or less. The effective daily dose is about 250 mg a day, if taken in a single dose. If taken in divided doses, 200 mg will be sufficient.

This dose is suitable (and recommended) for pregnant and breast-feeding women. The beta glucans are also indicated for infants, at 2.5 mg/kg bodyweight.

- Combining Forces

When your beta glucan-enhanced immune cells kill off pathogens, they use various anti-microbial tools to do this. One of these is hydrogen peroxide. This activates the innate immune enzyme lactoperoxidase, which is also very good at killing germs; so it makes good sense to ensure that your lactoperoxidase also has what it needs in order to work well. See Chapter 4C for details.

Food sources of beta glucans include yeast and mushrooms. The beta glucans in mushrooms are significantly less effective, and are best regarded as partial agonists (117).

Natural immuno-enhancers

B. Prebiotics, probiotics and the microbiome

Prebiotic fibres are an essential component in our diet. They are as important for our health as vitamins. Unlike classical micronutrients such as the vitamins, however, we do not use the fibres directly. They are food for our microbiome, the huge, complex and shifting colony of microorganisms that live inside us, mostly in the large bowel. In particular, they are food for probiotic species of bacteria such as lactobacilli and bifidobacteria, the species that are found in yoghurt or kefir. The more prebiotic fibre you eat, the more these health-promoting probiotic bacteria thrive inside us, and as they grow they displace and kill off other species of potentially harmful bacteria. This is a very positive thing to do. The shift to a healthier microbiome reduces inflammation in the intestines and is associated with many benefits locally, in the gut, and elsewhere in the body. According to the World Health Organisation, doubling our fibre intake reduces the risk of death from all causes by around 30% (2).

Unfortunately, while traditional diets contained large amounts of these fibres, they have been largely removed from today's processed, industrial human fodder; the average diet today barely reaches half of the W.H.O. recommended intake (2, 64). This undoubtedly contributes to our appallingly bad public health, and explains why it is so important to increase your intake of prebiotics.

Now we come back to immune health.

> *A healthier microbiome protects against heart disease, cancer and diabetes, and it also reduces the risk of infection.*

This is because the microbiome is not only a key metabolic nexus, but also a highly important part of our innate immune system. If the probiotic species in your microbiome are thriving, they kill off and crowd out other, harmful microbes, which might otherwise cause serious infections. Probiotics such as lactobacilli use four different strategies to do this.

1. They up-regulate the local immune system, helping it to fight off pathogens.
2. They 'steal' nutrients from disease-causing microbes, and dislodge them from their binding sites in the gut.
3. They break down prebiotic fibers into benign fatty acids, reducing intestinal pH which further discourages pathogen growth and may interfere with their quorum sensing (65). (See section on quorum sensing, Chapter 4F).
4. They produce anti-microbial compounds including ethanol, hydrogen peroxide and a range of bacteriocins. These do no harm to us, but they do kill off many harmful species of microbe (66-70) including the dreaded (and highly lethal) Carbapenem-Resistant Enterobacteriaceae (71).

The probiotic bacteria are very important to our health indeed, which is why prebiotic fibers are so very protective.

As the contents of the intestine are constantly moving, you need prebiotic fibres with different molecular structures in order to support the growth of probiotic species in different parts of the intestine. An ideal blend would contain small amounts of a fast-acting fibre such as fructo-oligosaccharide (FOS), and progressively larger doses of a moderately fast-acting fibre such as inulin, a slow fiber such as 1-3, 1-4 beta glucan and a very slow fibre such as resistant starch. Using this kind of blend, the microbiome can be renewed throughout the large bowel.

FOS and inulin are typically derived from chicory root, 1-3, 1-4 beta glucans from oats, and resistant starch can be obtained from green bananas or potato that has been repeatedly cooked and then cooled. (1-3, 1-4 beta glucans from oats are different from the 1-3, 1-6 beta glucans from yeast.)

The entry level dose of blended prebiotic fibres is at least 5 g/day. The available science indicates that a dose of 10 g/day will provide further protection.

Food sources of prebiotic fibers include Jerusalem artichokes, oats, green bananas, twice-cooked potatoes, legumes and pulses.

Natural immuno-enhancers

C. Lactoperoxidase; one enzyme, two nutrient requirements

Lactoperoxidase (LPO) may not be very familiar, but it is probably the most important enzyme component in the innate immune system. It protects the eyes, ears, nose and throat; the gastrointestinal, respiratory and genitourinary tracts, and the mammary glands. When an infection occurs, innate immune cells such as neutrophils attack the pathogen and produce hydrogen peroxide. The lactoperoxidase enzyme reacts to the presence of hydrogen peroxide by producing hypothiocyanite and hypoiodite ions, which are very effective indeed at killing disease-causing bacteria and fungi, and preventing viral infection.

There are just two problems.

LPO is a ferro-protein, which means that it requires iron in order to function. In order to make hypoiodite it requires iodine from the diet, and in order to make hypothiocyanite ions it also requires cyanogens which, like iron and iodine, must be obtained from the diet. Cyanogens include cyanogenic glycosides from cereals such as millet, and glucosinolates from brassica vegetables like broccoli, cabbage and brussels sprouts. Unfortunately, iron depletion is the single most common form of malnutrition, our intakes of cyanogens are at an historical low and in many countries iodine levels are falling – so this all-important enzyme often cannot function properly.

Any immune-enhancing regime should contain iron, if it is known to be needed, iodine and a cyanogen such as an extract from broccoli. I have found that this approach, when combined with 1-3, 1-6 beta glucans and prebiotic fibers, provides comprehensive protection.

In persons who are already feeling unwell, LPO can be used in a different and amplified way. Already used to preserve bulk milk, the enzyme can be obtained in powder form and made to work its magic in vitro. Once you add a cyanogen, and the enzyme has produced the hypothiocyanite effector ions, the resulting solution can be drunk. It looks and tastes just like water.

The range of conditions that benefit from this kind of LPO amplification is truly remarkable. Equally importantly, this approach has no adverse effects

– it does not, for example, damage the probiotic species in our microbiome. This is hardly surprising. The LPO system was designed and refined over many millions of years by nature and by evolution, unlike today's very recently developed antimicrobial drugs.

LPO amplification, available as KIB500*, is completely safe and highly and rapidly effective.

Food sources of cyanogens include brassica vegetables (including cabbage, kale, broccoli, brussels sprouts, cress, kohlrabi, turnip); and apple pips, sorghum, bitter almonds and lima beans.

---

*For further information: **www.kib.uk.com**
For ordering by or via healthcare practitioners: **www.kib500.com**

Natural immuno-enhancers

D. Anti-adhesins

Fucoidans and funorans, which occur in edible seaweeds, are nature's teflon. Their non-stick properties prevent disease-causing bacteria from adhering to sites in the body where they would otherwise multiply and cause problems. For this reason, the fucoidans and funorans are termed anti-adhesins. The best-documented site where they protect us is in the mouth. A number of studies have shown that consuming seaweed extract prevents bacteria from adhering to the teeth, reduces plaque and tartar, and protects against gum disease and dental erosion (72).

There is another type of infection where these marine compounds may be life-saving. Numbers of people with prosthetic hips, knees and heart valves are increasing rapidly, and one thing all these implants have in common is that they are not immuno-competent. I have heard from colleagues of sudden deaths occurring years after surgery in such patients. After other causes had been excluded, in many cases autopsy revealed biofilm and other signs of infection on the prosthesis. The surgeon who originally implanted the prosthesis is unaware of this problem, as it can occur many years after surgery. This may reflect very slow-growing infections, or it may be to do with cumulative risk over time. Potentially pathogenic bacteria exist in all tissues, including the brain and bloodstream, and a temporary dip in immunity may be enough to allow a prosthetic infection to begin.

> *Antibiotics cannot be prescribed for decade-long prophylaxis. Natural anti-adhesins such as the fucoidans and funorans are safe, however, and in my view likely to be protective.*

There are other natural anti-adhesins. The best known is the sugar D-mannose, which can be used to displace pathogens from the urinary tract (73, 74). Less well known (and less well characterised) are the sugars produced when the carbohydrates in carrot are hydrolysed. These are formed when carrot soup is prepared, providing it is boiled for long enough to allow the slight sweetness of the sugars to emerge.

Carrot soup is a traditional treatment for gastro-intestinal problems; and while carrot contains anti-bacterial compounds (75), my best guess is that carrot sugars have the ability to displace probiotic species from the small bowel where they should not be, and where they can cause problems. This condition is known as small intestinal bacterial overgrowth, or SIBO. The carrot cure is, in my limited experience, faster and more effective than the FODMAP diet.

Microbiologists and infection specialists have recently described anti-adhesin therapy as effective in the prevention and treatment of bacterial infections (76). This new infection control strategy will eventually percolate through to medical practice, but almost certainly in the form of synthetic, patented and over-expensive drugs with doubtful safety profiles. The natural compounds listed above are safe, and seem to be effective enough.

Sialic acid, a common constituent in many foods, appears to be able to interfere with viral docking and so may help to protect against certain viral infections (77). This has a folk medicine background. In some areas, mothers have traditionally splashed a drop of breast milk into a snotty baby's nose to help it get over a cold, and some speculate that the milk's high content of sialic acid is what makes this effective. However, it is equally possible that the lactoperoxidase in milk is responsible for the anti-viral effect; and while breast milk is obviously safe, there are some safety concerns about the long-term use of sialic acids from non-human sources (78). This story is developing.

In the meantime, the Stockholm-based company Avia Pharma AB has launched the sialic acid nasal spray 'Viral', for short-term use. Initial results are extremely positive (79).

Food sources of fucoidans and funorans include the edible kelps ascophyllum nodosum (Norwegian kelp), wakame and kombu.

Natural immuno-enhancers

E. Quorum sensor inhibitors

Once a pathogenic microbe has accessed an environment in the body where it has an opportunity to grow, it does not cause problems right away. It tries not to call attention to itself too early, alerting the immune system before it is present in sufficient numbers to overcome host defences. Bacteria 'talk' to each other using chemical messages, and it is only when levels of these messenger substances are high enough that the bacteria, sensing that they have reached a critical threshold, become virulent. This is called 'Quorum sensing'. Anthrax is a good example. When anthrax bacilli first invade they start to multiply, but do not produce anthrax toxin until they reach a threshold number of bacteria.

This provides another opportunity to reduce our chances of infection, because a number of natural compounds interfere with quorum sensing and prevent the emergence of virulence. Quorum-sensor inhibitors occur in vanilla, clove, ginger, cardamon, horseradish, garlic and dill (80 - 86), These compounds tip the balance against infection (87, 88) and I recommend

regular doses of such spices, plus the anti-adhesins described above, to patients with artificial hips, knees or heart valves.

Nicotine has the opposite effect; it enhances bacterial quorum sensing (89) and can make bacteria more virulent (90). This helps to explain why smokers get more infections, and provides yet another reason why smoking is bad for your health.

Food sources of quorum sensor inhibitors include vanilla, clove, ginger, cardamom, horseradish, garlic and dill.

Natural immuno-enhancers

F. Vitamin D and selenium

Vitamin D. Recommended: vitamin D3, 250 mcg/day (=10,000 IU).

In the European and US temperate zones, most people are depleted in vitamin D for most of the year. This is not bad enough to cause rickets, but it has been identified as a contributory factor to the common problems of osteoporosis and osteopenia. More recently, vitamin D depletion has also been shown to reduce the effectiveness of the innate immune system.

A gene called Vitamin D3-Upregulated Protein 1 (VDUP1) plays a crucial role in directing stem cells to diversify into natural killer cells, one of the key elements in the innate immune system. One of their functions is to eliminate virus-infected cells. If you are low in vitamin D fewer NK-cells are formed, and your innate immune defences against viruses become impaired. As the other function of NK-cells is to kill tumour cells, D-depletion probably increases the risk of cancer also.

> *Adequate vitamin D intakes are extremely important.*

The current UK RDA for vitamin D is only 5mcg, with the US advising 10 mcg day for the over 50's. The current UK official upper safe limit is set, somewhat arbitrarily, at only 25 mcg. There are ongoing discussions about increasing this upper safe limit. It has already been increased to 50 mcg in the USA, but is likely to be set still higher. In 2011 the American Institute of Medicine determined that the highest safe dose was 250µg vitamin D/day, and set an upper limit at 100 mcg /day.

To put this in context, leading experts in this area state that 500 mcg a day is a safe and effective dose. This assessment is based on the existing safety and toxicity data, and on the fact that in any sub-tropical region you will make 500 mcg vitamin D3 in your own body by walking around in the sun without a shirt on for an hour or so (91).

<u>Selenium.</u> Recommended – 150 mcg/day, as methylselenocysteine.

Selenium deficiency allows invading viruses to mutate and remain for a longer period in the host (92, 93). Researchers at the University of North Carolina in Chapel Hill compared mice that received a selenium-deficient diet with non-deficient animals, all of which were exposed to the human influenza virus. The deficient mice had more severe cases of the flu that lasted for a longer period of time than in the non-deficient mice.

Selenium depletion is prevalent in large parts of the world, including the UK (94). Accordingly, here is another dietary factor contributing to an increased risk of infection – and, possibly, cancer (95).

RDA values range between 30 and 55 mcg/day, but I believe that these are also sub-optimal. 150 mcg/day seems to be adequate in most cases. This is well within the safe range, which extends to 800 mcg (94).

Food sources of selenium include brazil nuts, and seafoods such as tuna, halibut, sardines and shrimp.

Food sources of vitamin D include salmon, herring, sardines, egg yolks and mushrooms. But the best source is sunlight.

Natural immuno-enhancers

G) Additional micro- and phytonutrients

The immune system has a wide range of nutrient requirements. As Type B malnutrition has become so prevalent, most people today would do well to invest in a comprehensive daily nutritional support program. This should at a minimum include optimal levels of the classical vitamins and minerals, together with a range of polyphenols, carotenoids and xanthophylls (derived from many fruits and vegetables), and the omega 3 fatty acids EPA and DHA. All these are required for good health. Most commercial A to Z formulations are restricted to the basic vitamins and minerals, and confer no benefits at all.

5. Autoimmunity

Autoimmune diseases are increasing, and the medical establishment has no good explanation for this.

Patients with autoimmune conditions such as rheumatoid arthritis, Type 1 diabetes, Graves, lupus and multiple sclerosis generally have antibodies in their bloodstream which target the affected tissues, and drive the chronic inflammation that causes progressive damage to the joint, pancreas, thyroid ... These antibodies are called autoantibodies.

Since women are up to three times more likely to suffer from autoimmune disease, it is thought that hormones may play a role. Genes are an important factor in some cases, and exposure to certain toxins may also be involved. As the incidence of many autoimmune diseases is rising by 3 – 4% per year (96), lifestyle factors are clearly also playing a role here. There is circumstantial but persuasive evidence that today's pro-industrial industrial diet is involved (97, 98).

The standard theory of autoimmune disease, which is half a century old, holds that autoantibodies are produced by an immune system that has gone awry; and the most popular version of this is the pathogen / trigger theory. The problem supposedly starts when an infection is caused by a specific pathogen which happens to carry, on its surface, a molecule that resembles a molecule that occurs in the host. This is called molecular mimicry (ie 99). The immune system produces antibodies to the molecule carried by the pathogen, kills off the infection but then continues to make antibodies against the similar molecule found in the host. This leads to chronic inflammation, and progressive tissue destruction.

Clinicians who believe this theory prescribe immunosuppressant drugs. These drugs reduce inflammation and earn the drug industry enormous amounts of money, but they are non-curative and extremely toxic. However, the pathogen / trigger theory may well be wrong. If so, this opens the door to forms of treatment which may be more appropriate, more effective and less dangerous.

When autoantibodies were first discovered, microbiology was still in its infancy. The microbiome had not been discovered and scientists of the day did not know, as we do now, that waves of microbes are constantly surging through the entire body. There are thousands of different microbes and pathogens continually ranging through all of our tissues (100), entire ecosystems that are dynamic, largely uncharacterized and mostly invisible. And what is now becoming clear is that many so-called autoantibodies are likely to be antibodies to pathogens that former test methods were unable to detect.

There are at least three major lines of evidence that undermine the old pathogen / trigger model. Firstly, many people have autoantibodies but do not have the symptoms of autoimmune disease. More convincingly, antibiotics which kill off certain types of pathogens have been shown to stop autoimmune disease (101). As many of the suspected pathogens are intra-cellular, the antibiotic course may need to be protracted. Conversely, certain antibiotics and other causes of dysbiosis increase the risk of autoimmunity (102, 103).

Many of the microbes implicated in autoimmune disease are oral and gastrointestinal species. This provides a plausible explanation for the ongoing increase in rheumatoid arthritis, type 1 diabetes, Grave's disease, lupus and similar conditions. Our increasingly ultra-processed diet is loaded with sugar. At the same time it is depleted in prebiotic fibres and most micro- and phytonutrients, and it causes chronic inflammation. It is a diet calculated to distort the microbiome and disrupt the immune system.

This lays the foundation for a new approach to autoimmune disease. I have seen remarkable responses to initial intervention with KIB500, followed by the use of maintenance dietary tools. These include reducing sugar intake, and the use of anti-adhesins, blended prebiotic fibres, 1-3, 1-6 beta glucans, and broad spectrum micro- and phytonutrient support. The results of this regime suggest that once the pathogens have been pushed back and the microbiome brought back to normal, 'molecular mimicry' is no longer an issue.

6. More ways to protect against viral and bacterial threats

a. Healthy eating

A large body of evidence indicates that the Mediterranean diet, which contains high levels of anti-inflammatory and prebiotic ingredients, not only lowers the risk of heart disease and cancer but also supports good immune function. This diet is high in fruits and vegetables, wholegrain, beans and other legumes, olive oil, nuts and seeds, garlic and fish. A modicum of red wine and dark chocolate is also included... But go easy on the salt. High salt intakes damage the immune system's ability to repel invading bacteria (104).

b. Adequate sleep

Getting enough sleep is important for general good health. Lack of sleep is perceived by the body as a form of stress, and can lead to a reduced immune response.

c. Exercise

Exercise is an effective immune booster and important for health generally. Being unfit is as bad for health as smoking 20 cigarettes a day. A program of regular, moderate exercise relieves stress and makes it easier to sleep at night. Excessive and intense, sustained exercise, however, can reduce immune responses. Marathon runners take note!

d. Other precautions:

Colds are not only transmitted through the air via coughing and sneezing, but also via surface contact - such as door handles. It makes sense to wash your hands regularly with soap and water and to avoid touching your eyes, nose or mouth.

Food preparation is another area where sensible precautions reduce the risk of food-borne infection such as gastroenteritis. Rinse meat and fish under running water before cooking, and wash your hands each time a new raw food is touched. Never cut cooked and raw meats on the same board, and ensure that any raw animal products are properly packed and stored on the lowest shelf in the fridge.

e. And another thing...

Stop smoking if you haven't already done so. Maintain a healthy weight, control blood pressure and drink alcohol in moderation. Two glasses of red wine per day seems about right. Use a stress reduction technique when appropriate.

7. Answers to (some of) your questions

Does being cold make you more likely to catch a cold?

Prolonged and severe cold exposure may reduce immune functions. However, colds and flu are more prevalent in the winter because cold weather means we spend more time indoors in closer contact with other people – and at a time when our vitamin D levels are at their lowest.

Can 1-3, 1-6 beta glucan trigger yeast infection or allergy?

Some people have concerns about yeast because they have heard that baker's yeast might increase the risk of candida infections. There is no truth in this story.

Others believe that they may be allergic to 1-3, 1-6 beta glucan, as it comes from yeast. Although allergy to yeast does occur, the immune reaction is to mannoproteins found on yeast cell walls. Purified beta glucan preparations are free of yeast protein and are hypo-allergenic. In fact, due to their secondary effects on the acquired immune system, they have significant anti-allergy effects.

Why is infection often accompanied by a fever?

A higher body temperature speeds up the workings of the body's immune cells, resulting in a more effective immune response. In addition, some micro organisms do not reproduce well at higher temperatures. This kind of fever is an important defence mechanism. Anti-pyretic (fever-reducing) drugs such as aspirin and ibuprofen should not be used immediately to treat fever, but only after a few hours of raised temperature. In this way the benefits of fever are retained. Cool or cold-water bathing is in many cases a better option.

Can antibiotics be counter-productive?

Antibiotics tend to knock out both the bad *and* the good flora – which can leave a vacancy for harmful bacteria to move in and flourish. In these circumstances, prebiotic fibres that promote the growth of the host's own probiotic species can be helpful. Alternatively, use LPO amplification. This will selectively remove pathogens while leaving probiotic species unharmed.

When should I give children antibiotics?

Children with sore throats should not be given antibiotics unless lab tests show a strep or other bacterial infection. Bronchitis or non-specific coughs rarely warrant antibiotics unless the symptoms last more than 10 days, and a particular bacterium is suspected; and in cases where there is an underlying lung disease such as cystic fibrosis (but not asthma).

Antibiotics should not be given for the common cold even when there is a nasal discharge, which is fairly normal. Short courses of antibiotics should be given for acute middle ear infections (otitis media), but they are not indicated for otitis media with effusion. This is a subtle but vital distinction which the doctor makes when he/she first sees the child.

If an antibiotic is effective against the bacterium on hand, and if it is going to do the job properly, it must be taken for the duration of the recommended course. Antibiotics don't work right away, and most children take a couple of days to start feeling better. Some parents assume that the drugs aren't working and stop after the first dose. Others stop once the child has started to improve, and do not finish the course. These actions greatly increase the risk of resistance developing; as does re-using antibiotics that may have been left over from a previous bout, or which belonged to someone else.

The problems of drug resistance cannot be left to the specialist infection control teams. We all have a responsibility to ensure antibiotics are used properly, and have an important role to play if we want to be able to continue to rely on these drugs when we really need them.

Are oat beta glucans the same as the beta glucans from yeast?

The 1-3, 1-6 beta glucans from yeast and the 1-3, 1-4 beta glucans derived from oats have subtly different molecular structures, and exert very different effects in the body.

1-3, 1-6 beta glucan, which binds to the CR3 receptor on immune cells, enhances innate immune function. 1-3, 1-4 beta glucan primarily acts as a prebiotic fibre in the gut, driving the growth of probiotic bacteria and, indirectly, lowering plasma cholesterol.

Appendix A: How 1-3, 1-6 beta glucans work

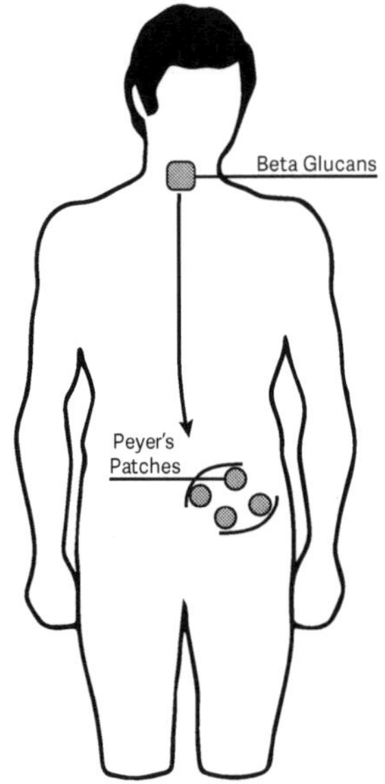

Figure 1

1. Once swallowed, whole beta glucan particles pass through the stomach into the small intestine where they are taken up by specialised intestinal cells called M-cells, in regions of the gut called Peyer's Patches (Fig 1). M-cells transport the beta glucan particles to circulating macrophages, circulating in the blood stream. Macrophages are innate immune cells whose function is to engulf and digest invading micro organisms.

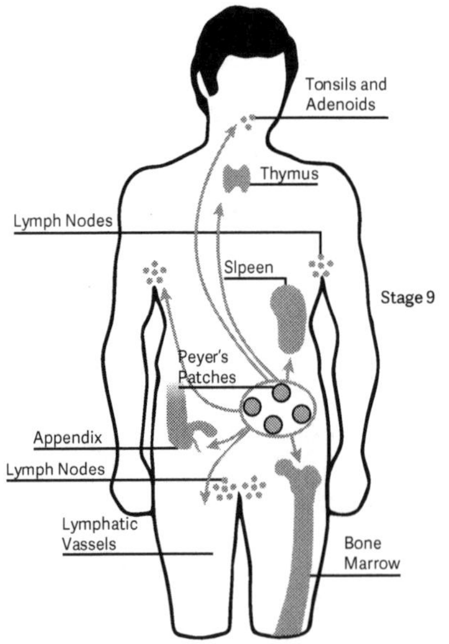

Figure 2

2. The macrophages convey the whole glucan particles to various regions of the immune system such as lymph nodes and bone marrow (Fig 2). As they travel they digest the beta glucan particles, breaking them down to smaller fragments which they spit out into the circulation in a timed-release manner, over a period of 24 – 36 hours. These active fragments bind onto the surface of neutrophils, the most abundant immune cells in the body.

Both macrophages and neutrophils have receptors which specifically recognise 1-3, 1-6 beta glucan (105) because this compound occurs in the cell walls of yeasts and other fungi which the immune system sees as a major threat. When you ingest beta glucan your innate immune system 'thinks' that an enemy has arrived and it rises to the challenge. This important first line of defence is now fully activated, and scientists have shown that resistance to infection (and possibly to cancer) is greatly enhanced (106 - 108).

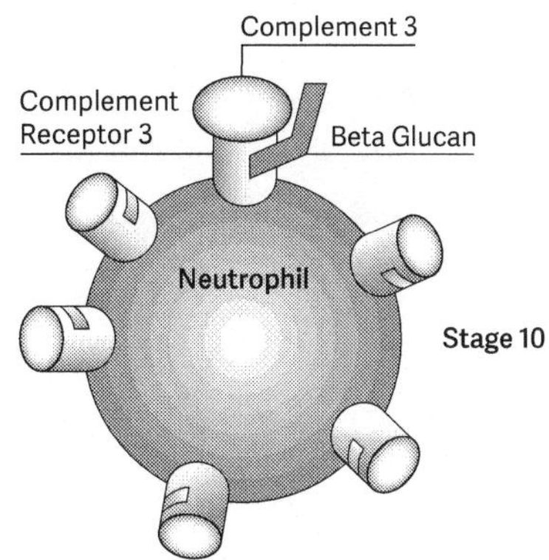

3. The receptor described above is called Complement Receptor 3 (CR3). When beta glucan fragments bind to CR3 receptors (Fig 3), the macrophages and neutrophils are now primed and ready to react to foreign challenges or pathogens. Neutrophils are the dominant cell type in this situation.

4. For a neutrophil to kill a pathogen, its CR3 receptor must be occupied by complement – a blood protein – and by beta glucan. The CR3 receptor is occupied naturally by beta glucan on the cell walls of moulds and yeasts. But there are other threats including bacteria, viruses and cancer, where, in our over-sterile environment, beta glucan is not present in sufficient amounts to allow an optimal immune response.

By taking a beta glucan supplement, the neutrophils are provided with the missing element they need to optimise their killing mechanism.

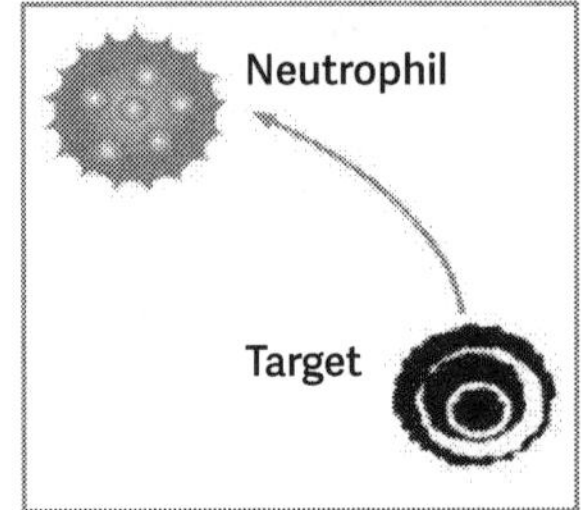

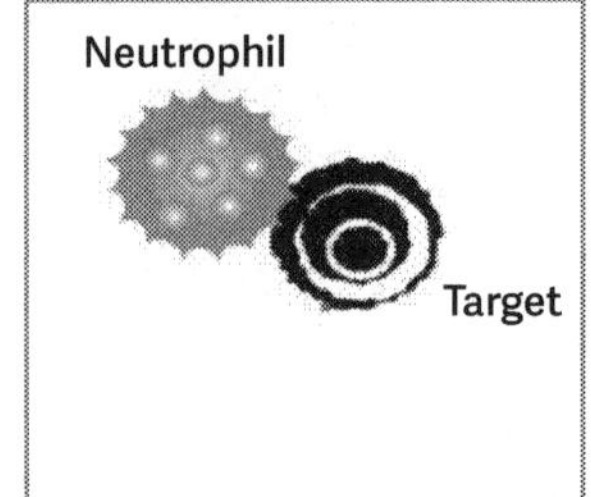

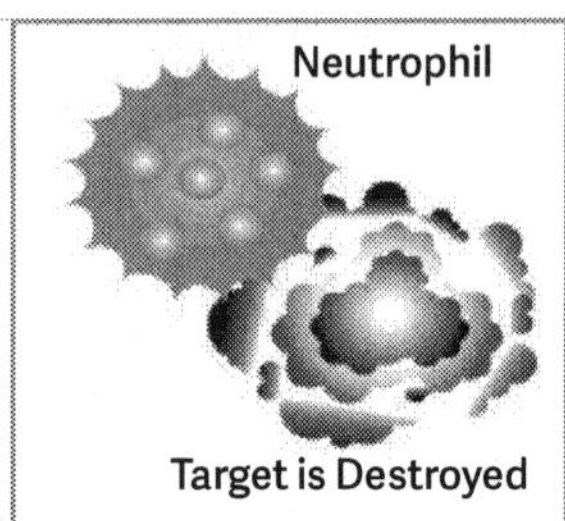

Figure 4a

Figure 4b

Figure 4c

5. A fully primed neutrophil now migrates to the site of its target (bacterium or cancer cell) through a process called chemotaxis. [fig 4a] The primed neutrophil binds to the target, recognizes it as 'non-self' ie foreign, and destroys it by releasing toxic chemicals [Figures 4b and 4c].

Other killer cells retain fragments of the pathogens they have destroyed and 'present' them on their surface. These fragments – called antigens – send signals to other members of the immune system family of cells, which become memory cells.

Next time the pathogen is encountered, these newly programmed memory cells will recognize it and produce antibodies. These antibodies stick to the surface of the pathogen and may destroy it, or prevent it from infecting healthy cells.

This is one way the innate immune system helps the adaptive immune system to work properly (see Appendix B).

Appendix B: The Adaptive Immune System

This is called the Adaptive Immune System because, after a first exposure to a pathogen it 'adapts' itself so that it can destroy that pathogen the next time it encounters it. Its main agents are lymphocytes (white blood cells), which are divided into B cells and T cells.

Both B and T cells are made in the bone marrow. B cells grow in the marrow but T cells move out and mature in the Thymus (hence T cells). When mature, both cells travel via the blood stream to secondary lymphoid tissues such as the lymph node, spleen, tonsils, adenoids, Peyer's patches and appendix. Some of these cells are relatively sedentary while others travel throughout the body.

There are thousands of different B and T cells, each created to recognize one particular antigen, the little piece of pathogen displayed on the surface of a phagocyte. The antigens in turn stimulate the release of chemical messengers called cytokines which tell B and T cells to ramp up their attack on the foreign virus or bacteria.

They do this by multiplying into a whole army of cloned cells, some of which become memory cells that ensure your immune system remembers each pathogen in future. This is why you will generally not catch the same infection twice.

Much of the time you are unaware of all this drama acting out in your body. At other times swelling, heat, itch, pain and inflammation tell you that B and T cells are multiplying in the area of infection.

Vaccines stimulate the Adaptive Immune System and give you immunity in a similar, but not as effective way as an authentic bacterial or viral attack. By inoculating you with a pathogen that has been inactivated, your B cells are stimulated to produce anti-bodies as if the attack were real, creating a 'pre-memory' of that yet-to-be encountered threat.

The process of vaccination was first developed by Edward Jenner in the late 18th Century when he noticed that milk maids – who were exposed to cow pox – rarely contracted the closely-related small pox. As Trivial Pursuiters and medical students know, the word vaccination comes from vacca, the Latin for cow.

Vaccines have become Big Pharma's most rapidly growing profit centre, and are projected to be worth $100 billion by 2025 (109). The vast sums of money to be made have encouraged major vaccine manufacturers to fake their data (110); but I am not against vaccination per se.

Some vaccines, such as polio vaccine, have an excellent therapeutic index. Others, however, are of more doubtful value. In the case of flu, for example, vaccines have only limited effectiveness against any specific strain of the virus. If the flu virus mutates, as it does from year to year, the previous vaccine may be rendered completely ineffective. And some vaccines have been linked to serious, albeit uncommon adverse effects (111).

These are more good arguments for optimising the innate immune system.

Allergy

Allergies are disorders where the adaptive immune system over-reacts to a normally harmless antigen like pollen or animal dander. That may cause a runny nose or sneezing, since many allergies are inhalation-related. In extreme cases the reaction can be a life-threatening anaphylactic shock, for example to peanuts.

An allergic reaction is essentially a cascade of interlinked cell-to-cell communications. Initially an allergen will bind to an IgE antibody which in turn binds to a type of immune cell called a mast cell, triggering it to release compounds called histamines. It is histamines that cause the symptoms of swelling, itching, runny eyes etc. These symptoms cause more inflammatory cells to gather at the site, a vicious circle that can damage tissue and lead to a chronic illness such as asthma. Current treatments include antihistamines, decongestants, anti-inflammatory agents and an anti-IgE drug called Omalizumab.

Allergy has increased hugely since 1950, and there is persuasive evidence that this is connected to the progressive removal of 1-3, 1-6 beta glucans from our diet. This creates an imbalance in the ratio of a sub-species of T-cells called T-Helper cells (TH-cells). Specifically, it has decreased the numbers of TH-1 cells, which are involved in long-term immunity to infection, and increased the numbers of TH-2 cells, which are deeply implicated in allergy. Putting 1-3, 1-6 beta glucans back in the diet restores the normal ratio of TH1 and TH2 cells (60), and reduces allergy very significantly (61).

Allergy involves and creates chronic inflammation, and anti-inflammatory pharmaco-nutritional tools can be extremely helpful. These are described in the companion book 'Let Your Food be your PharmacoNutrition', available from Amazon.com and Zinzino.com. Further articles are freely available from **www.drpaulclayton.eu**

These anti-inflammatory tools are also very helpful in dealing with the symptoms of autoimmune disease.

Appendix C: Viral epidemics - and Wuhan (Covid-19)

Due to our political masters' nightmarish desire for a global marketplace for cheap goods (for us) and cheap and docile labour (for them), pandemics such as the current coronavirus will continue to wash across the world. How can we protect ourselves?

Social distancing, masks, disposable gloves and hand-washing are all useful preventative strategies, but there are a few more tools we can use. Sialic acid sprays such as Viral Nose Spray may offer an additional chance of preventing infection. If you find yourself in a vulnerable situation (crowds, obviously ill individuals etc), I recommend using the spray intra-nasally, in the mouth and across the eyes, as the virus can gain entry to the body via any of these portals.

To understand which other nutritional tools might be useful in managing Covid-19, we have to go back to the basic epidemiology and time course of the disease.

Around 90% of individuals known to be infected suffer no or only minor symptoms and do not require hospitalization (112). The percentage may actually be higher, if there are large numbers of undiagnosed and asymptomatic cases still to be discovered; but let's use that 90% figure for now. What determines whether you will be in the 90% who recover, or the 10 % who don't?

The size of inoculum probably plays a role, ie the numbers of viruses that an individual is exposed to. Risk factors such as age, obesity, smoking, vaping, air pollution, the use of ACE-2 inhibitors and comorbidities such as diabetes, hypertension and lung and kidney disease are important. But there is more. The timing of the disease stages indicates that functionality of the innate immune system is pivotal.

The disease begins with a virusaemia lasting 7 to 9 days, which is associated with relatively nonspecific symptoms such as nasal discharge, sore throat and mild fever. The patient then reaches a fork in the road. In most cases he or she recovers because the innate immune system has successfully overcome the viral challenge; at that stage the adaptive immune system is still pulling its boots on. In approximately 15% of cases however the innate immune system fails to contain the virus and the disease progresses to a mixed viral and bacterial pneumonia, and finally to a mixed viral, bacterial and fungal pneumonia. The innate and adaptive immune systems now become dysfunctional, and inflammation overwhelms the patient.

If innate immune function could be improved, the impact on healthcare requirements would be considerable. Improving from an 90/10 split to a 95/5 split would cut the need for intensive hospital care in half.

It is known that the coronavirus is quickly rendered ineffective by relatively low concentrations of hydrogen peroxide and hypochlorous acid, and by hypothiocyanite and hypoiodite ions. Innate immune cells produce hydrogen peroxide and hypochlorous acid when challenged, and do so more effectively when primed with 1-3, 1-6 beta glucans. Hypoiodite and hypothiocyanite ions are produced by the immune enzyme LPO, which can generate more of these when supplied with iron, and iodine and cyanogens, the enzyme's cofactor and substrates respectively. So we should be well defended.

Unfortunately, the modern diet damages both our immune cells and the immune enzyme LPO. Iron depletion is the single most common form of dysnutrition today, and dietary intakes of 1-3, 1-6 beta glucans, iodine and cyanogens have declined markedly over the last century or so (5). Vitamin D and the trace element selenium, both of which are essential for interferon activity (113, 114, are at low levels also; as is zinc, which has the ability to reduce coronavirus replication (115). These negative dietary changes have degraded the functionality of the innate immune system, and provide a rationale for widespread dietary supplementation programs.

The effectiveness of such composite nutritional interventions are not yet proven but they are supported by circumstantial evidence and unlike the pharmaceutical approaches, they have very wide therapeutic indices. This makes them eminently suitable for general usage, and for consideration in preventative and interventional public health strategies.

Exogenous LPO may be an effective treatment on its own. There is circumstantial but persuasive evidence that the LPO system has the ability, if it is working well, to damage influenza and probably coronaviruses to the point where they cannot infect new cells in the body (116-121, 123). In infected subjects who are already in the second stage of the disease, temporary amplification of LPO activity via KIB500 may enable the viral challenge to be reduced to the point where the patient's basic functions can be restored.

Under current regulatory legislation, it is illegal to recommend any non-pharmaceutical treatment for a disease state. This legislation is a medical Maginot Line, a hopelessly outdated framework which is more to do with protecting the interests of Big Pharma than preserving or improving public health. I cannot, therefore, say that KIB500 is a treatment for the current epidemic, or indeed any flu. What I will say, however, is that if I or anyone I cared for were to be diagnosed with such an illness, I would use KIB50 to manage my own symptoms.

Footnote. The anti-malarial drugs chloroquine and hydroxychloroquine are emerging as possible treatments for Covid-19, and if early reports are substantiated this is good news for everyone.

Viruses are good at developing drug resistance, as we saw with oseltamivir (Tamiflu); and this may be only a temporary respite. Better public nutrition will continue to be a bulwark against most diseases.

Appendix D: Glossary

B-cell. A type of cell found in the adaptive immune system. It manufactures antibodies, but has other functions also.

Candida auris. A species of yeast considered to be a serious global health threat. Often acquired in hospitals, it is highly drug-resistant.

Carotenoids. Plant pigments responsible for red, yellow and orange hues in many fruits and vegetables; such as lycopene, found in tomatoes. They confer multiple health benefits.

CR3 receptor. A pattern recognition receptor carried by all immune cells, which recognizes various molecules found on the surface of different pathogens. Binding to this receptor triggers a sequence of events that leads to the death of the pathogen.

CRE. Bacteria such as E coli and Klebsiella species, a normal part of the microbiome in the gut, that have become resistant to the carbapenem antibiotics. They are very hard to treat, and have a high mortality rate.

FODMAP. Stands for Fermentable Oligosaccharides, Disaccharides, Monosaccharides and -Polyols. These compounds have prebiotic activity. Normally health-promoting, they cause problems if probiotic species have moved into the small bowel.

Fucoidans. Complex, sulphated polysaccharides that occur in many brown seaweeds. Have anti-adhesin and other useful properties.

Funorans. Related to fucoidan, and have similar properties.

Macrophage. An important part of the innate immune system. Engulfs and devours pathogens.

Monosaccharide. A sugar that cannot be broken down into a simpler sugar. Glucose and fructose are two examples.

MRSA. Strains of Staph aureus, often carried in the nose, that can break away and start infections in other tissues. Hard to treat, due to multiple antibiotic resistance.

Natural Killer cell. One of the cell types in the innate immune system. Can kill tumour cells and some virally infected cells.

Neutrophil. Another innate immune cell, and the most numerous one. It helps heal damaged tissues and resolve infections.

Oligosaccharide. A carbohydrate whose molecules are composed of a relatively small number of monosaccharide units.

Pathogen / pathogenic. Capable of causing disease.

Phytonutrients. Substances found in plants, usually food plants, believed to be beneficial to human health and help prevent various diseases. Examples are carotenoids, xanthophylls and polyphenols.

Polyphenol. A group of phytonutrients originally identified as Vitamin P, by the Hungarian chemist Albert Szent-Györgyi. They have significant anti-inflammatory and other benefits.

Polysaccharide. A carbohydrate such as starch whose molecules consist of long chains of monosaccharide units.

Prebiotic fiber. A carbohydrate found in pulses, legumes etc that cannot be digested, and passes intact into the large bowel where it fuels the growth of healthy, probiotic bacteria.

T-cell. One of two different types of cell in the adaptive immune system. Its main role is to determine the specific immune response to antigens.

TDRTB. Totally Drug-Resistant TB.

Therapeutic Index (TI). A ratio that compares the blood concentration at which a compound becomes toxic and the concentration at which it is effective. The larger the therapeutic index (TI), the safer the compound is. Nutrients usually have far greater TI's than drugs.

Ultra-processed food. Snacks, drinks, ready meals and many other product types formulated mostly or entirely from substances extracted from foods or derived from food constituents. These foods contain few if any recognizable ingredients, and often have an abnormally long shelf-life.

VRSA. Strains of Staph aureus resistant to Vancomycin.

Xanthophyll. Yellow or brown carotenoid plant pigments which cause the autumn colours of leaves. Some (ie lutein) are critical to the function of tissues in the body such as the retina.

Appendix E: References

1. Xie Y, Bowe B, Yan Y, Xian H, Li T, Al-Aly Z. **Estimates of all-cause mortality and cause specific mortality associated with proton pump inhibitors among US veterans: cohort study.** BMJ. 2019 May 29;365:l1580.
2. Reynolds A, Mann J, Cummings J, Winter N, Mete E, Te Morenga L. **Carbohydrate quality and human health: a series of systematic reviews and meta-analyses.** Lancet. 2019 Feb 2;393(10170):434-445.
3. Kempker JA, Martin GS. **A global accounting of sepsis.** Lancet. 2020 Jan 18;395(10219):168-170.
4. GBD 2013 Risk Factors Collaborators et al. **Global, regional, and national comparative risk assessment of 79 behavioural, environmental and occupational, and metabolic risks or clusters of risks in 188 countries, 1990-2013: a systematic analysis for the Global Burden of Disease Study 2013.** Lancet. 2015 Dec 5;386(10010):2287-323.
5. Clayton P, Rowbotham J. **How the mid-Victorians worked, ate and died.** Int J Environ Res Public Health. 2009 Mar;6(3):1235-53.
6. Kearney J. **Food consumption trends and drivers.** Philos Trans R Soc Lond B Biol Sci. 2010 Sep 27;365(1554):2793-807.
7. Fiolet T, Srour B, Sellem L, Kesse-Guyot E, Allès B, Méjean C, Deschasaux M, Fassier P, Latino-Martel P, Beslay M, Hercberg S, Lavalette C, Monteiro CA, Julia C, Touvier M. **Consumption of ultra-processed foods and cancer risk: results from NutriNet-Santé prospective cohort.** BMJ. 2018 Feb 14;360:k322.
8. Blanco-Rojo R, Sandoval-Insausti H, López-Garcia E, Graciani A, Ordovás JM, Banegas JR, Rodríguez-Artalejo F, Guallar-Castillón P. **Consumption of Ultra-Processed Foods and Mortality: A National Prospective Cohort in Spain.** Mayo Clin Proc. 2019 Nov;94(11):2178-2188.
9. Rico-Campà A, Martínez-González MA, Alvarez-Alvarez I, Mendonça RD, de la Fuente-Arrillaga C, Gómez-Donoso C, Bes-Rastrollo M. **Association between consumption of ultra-processed foods and all-cause mortality: SUN prospective cohort study.** BMJ. 2019 May 29;365:l1949.
10. Seong SK, Kim HW. **Potentiation of Innate Immunity by β-Glucans.** Mycobiology. 2010 Jun;38(2):144-8.
11. Gallagher-Allred CR, Voss AC, Finn SC, McCamish MA. **Malnutrition and clinical outcomes: the case for medical nutrition therapy.** J Am Diet Assoc 1996 Apr;96(4):361-6, 369.
12. Bistrian BR, Blackburn GL, Vitale J, Cochran D, Naylor J. **Prevalence of malnutrition in general medical patients.** JAMA 1976 Apr 12;235(15):1567-70.
13. Naber TH, **Schermer T, de Bree A, Nusteling K, Eggink L, Kruimel JW, Bakkeren J, van Heereveld H, Katan MB. Prevalence of malnutrition in nonsurgical hospitalized patients and its association with disease complications.** Am J Clin Nutr 1997 Nov;66(5):1232-9.
14. Bogden J. **Daily micronutrient supplements enhance delayed-hypersensitivity skin test responses in older people.** Am J Clin Nutr 1994; 60:437-447
15. Nyquist AC, Gonzales R, Steiner JF, Sande MA. **Antibiotic prescribing for children with colds, upper respiratory tract infections, and bronchitis.** JAMA. 1998 Mar 18;279(11):875-7.
16. CDC 1998: **Prescribing Guidelines.** *Pediatrics* 1998; 101:163—184
17. CFR 2019. **https://www.cfr.org/backgrounder/end-antibiotics**
18. Normile D. **Infectious diseases. Genetic analyses suggest bird flu virus is evolving.** Science. 2005 May 27;308(5726):1234-5.
19. ECDC Influenza Team. **H5N1 virus resistant to oseltamivir isolated from Vietnamese patient.** Euro Surveill. 2005 Oct 20;10(10):E051020.2.

20. Kernodle DS, Gates H, Kaiser AB. **Prophylactic anti-infective activity of poly-[1-6]-beta-D-glucopyranosyl-[1-3]-beta-D-glucopryanose glucan in a guinea pig model of staphylococcal wound infection.** Antimicrob Agents Chemother. 1998 Mar;42(3):545-9.

21. Wakshull E, Brunke-Reese D, Lindermuth J, Fisette L, Nathans RS, Crowley JJ, Tufts JC, Zimmerman J, Mackin W, Adams DS. **PGG-glucan, a soluble beta-(1,3)-glucan, enhances the oxidative burst response, microbicidal activity, and activates an NF-kappa B-like factor in human PMN: evidence for a glycosphingolipid beta-(1,3)-glucan receptor.** Immunopharmacology. 1999 Feb;41(2):89-107.

22. Mansell PWA, Ichinose I-I, Reed RJ, Krements ET, McNamee RB, Di Luzio NR: **Macrophage-mediated destruction of human malignant cells in vivo.** J Nat Cancer Inst 1975; 54: 571-580.

23. Hahn MG, Albersheim P: **Host-pathogen interactions. XIV. Isolation and partial characterization of an elicitor from yeast extract.** Plant Physiol 1978; 62: 107.

24. Robertsen B, Engstad RE, Jorgensen JB. **Beta- glucans as Immunostimulants in fish.** Immune Responses I994, V. 1 Fair Haven, NJ, USA.

25. Song Y-L, Hsieh Y-T. **Immunostimulation of tiger shrimp hemocytes for generation of microbicidal substances: analysis of reactive oxygen species.** Developmental and Comparative immunology, Vol.I, No.3, pp.201-209, 1994.Elsevier Science.

26. Rasmussen LT, Konopski Z, Oian P, Seljelid R. **Killing of Escherichia coli by mononuclear phagocytes and neutrophils stimulated in vitro with beta-1, 3-D-polyglucose derivatives,** Microbiol Immunol 36(11):1173-1188. 1992.

27. Rasmussen LT, Seljelid R. **Dynamics of blood components and peritoneal fluid during treatment of murine E. coli sepsis with beta-1, 3-D-polyglucose derivatives. I: Cells.** Scand J Immunol 32(4): 321-331. Oct 1990.

28. Rasmussen LT, Seljelid R. **Dynamics of blood components and peritoneal fluid during treatment of murine E. coli sepsis with beta-1, 3-D-polyglucose derivatives. II. Interleukin 1, tumor necrosis factor, prostaglandin E2 and leukotriene B4,** Scand J Immunol 32(4): 333-340. Oct 1990.

29. Rasmussen LT, Seljelid R. **The modulatory effect of lipoproteins on the release of interleukin 1 by human peritoneal macrophages stimulated with beta 1 -3D-polyglucose derivatives.** Scand J Immunol 1989; 29: 477-484.

30. Rasmussen LT, Seljelid R. **Production of prostaglandin E2 and interleukin 1 by mouse peritoneal macrophages stimulated with beta-1, 3-D-glucan derivatized plastic beads** Scand J Immunol 26(6): 731-736. Dec 1987.

31. Rasmussen, LT, Fandrem Jr, Seljelid R. **Dynamics of Blood Components and Peritoneal Fluid During Treatment of Murine E. Coli Sepsis with beta-1, 3-D-polyglucose Derivatives;** Scand. J Immunol 63:73-80 1985.

32. Williams DL, Diluzio NR. **Glucan-Induced Modification of murine Viral Hepatitis.** Science (1980), 208: 67-69. 1980.

33. Williams DL, Cook JA, Hoffmann EO, Di Luzio NR. **Protective Effect of Glucan in Experimentally Induced Candidiasis.** J. Reticuloendothel; Soc 23: 479-490. 1978.

34. Williams DL, Diluzio NR. **Glucan induced modification of experimental Staphylococcus aureus infection in normal, leukemic and immunosuppressed mice.** Adv Exp Med Biol 121(A): 291-306. 1979

35. Di Luzio NR, Williams DL. **The role of glucan in the prevention and modification of microparasitic diseases.** In: Assessments of chemical regulation of immunity in veterinary medicine. Gainer JH, ed. NY: Scientific, Medical and Scholarly Pub., 1983

36. Lahnborg G, Hedstrom KG, Nord CE. **The effect of glucan - a host resistance activator - and ampicillin on experimental intra-abdominal sepsis.** J Reticuloendothelial Soc 1982; 32: 347-353.

37. Leibovich SJ, Danon D. **Promotion of wound repair in mice by application of glucan.** J Reticuloendothelial Soc 1980; 27: 1-11.

38. Tzianabos AO, Cisneros RL. **Prophylaxis with the immunomodulator PGG glucan enhances antibiotic efficacy in rats infected with antibiotic-resistant bacteria,** Ann NY Acad Sci 797: 285-287; Oct 1996.

39. Rasmussen LT, Seljelid R. **Novel Immunomodulators With Pronounced In Vitro Effects Caused by Stimulation of Cytokine Release,** J Cell Biochem; 46:60-68. 1991.

40. Bowers GJ, Patchen ML, MacVittie TJ, Hirsch EF, Fink MP. **Glucan enhances survival in an intraabdominal infection model.** J Surg Res. 1989 Aug;47(2):183-8.

41. Patchen M. Alpha Beta Technology, 1997

42. Tzianabos AO, Cisneros RL. **Prophylaxis with the immunomodulator PGG glucan enhances antibiotic efficacy in rats infected with antibiotic-resistant bacteria.** Ann N Y Acad Sci. 1996 Oct 25;797:285-7.

43. Kaiser AB, Kernodle DS. **Synergism between poly-(1-6)-beta-D-glucopyranosyl-(1-3)-beta-D-glucopyranose glucan and cefazolin in prophylaxis of staphylococcal wound infection in a guinea pig model.** Antimicrob Agents Chemother. 1998 Sep;42(9):2449-51.

44. **Kournikakis B, Mandeville R, Brousseau P, Ostroff G. Anthrax-protective effects of yeast beta 1,3 glucans. MedGenMed.** 2003 Mar 21;5(1):1.

45 Mandeville R. Biophage Pharma Inc.

46. Jung K, Ha Y, Ha SK, Han DU, Kim DW, Moon WK, Chae C: **Antiviral effect of Saccharomyces cerevisiae beta-glucan to swine influenza virus by increased production of interferon-gamma and nitric oxide.** J Vet Med B Infect Dis Vet Public Health. 2004 Mar;51(2):72-6.

47. de Felippe J J, da Rocha-Silva F M, Maciel FM, Soares A de M, Mendes NF: **Infection prevention in patients with severe multiple trauma with the immunomodulator beta 1-3 polyglucose (glucan).** Surgery, Gynecology and Obstetrics 1993; 177(4): 383-388.

48. Babineau TJ, Hackford A, Kenler A, Bistrian B, Forse RA, Fairchild PG, Heard S, Keroack M, Caushaj P, Benotti P. **A phase II multicenter, double-blind, randomized, placebo-controlled study of three dosages of an immunomodulator (PGG-glucan) in high-risk surgical patients.** Arch Surg. 1994 Nov;129(11):1204-10.

49. Babineau TJ, Marcello P, Swails W, Kenler A, Bistrian B, Forse RA. **Randomized phase I/II trial of a macrophage-specific immunomodulator (PGG-glucan) in high-risk surgical patients.** Ann Surg. 1994 Nov;220(5):601-9.

50. Dellinger EP, Babineau TJ, Bleicher P, Kaiser AB, Seibert GB, Postier RG, Vogel SB, Norman J, Kaufman D, Galandiuk S, Condon RE. **Effect of PGG-glucan on the rate of serious postoperative infection or death observed after high-risk gastrointestinal operations. Betafectin Gastrointestinal Study Group.** Arch Surg. 1999 Sep;134(9):977-83.

51. Patchen ML, McVittie TJ: **Stimulated hemopoesis and enhanced survival following glucan treatment in sublethally and lethally irradiated mice.** Int J Immunopharmac 1985; 7: 923-932.

52. Patchen ML, D'Alesandro MM, Brook I, Blakely WF, McVittie TJ: **Glucan: mechanisms involved in its "radioprotective" effect.** J Leuc Biol 1987; 42: 95-105.

53. Patchen ML, MacVittie TJ, Brook I. **Glucan-induced hemopoietic and immune stimulation: therapeutic effects in sublethally and lethally irradiated mice.** Methods Find Exp Clin Pharmacol. 1986 Mar;8(3):151-5.

54. Burikhanov RB, Wakame K, Igarashi Y, Wang S, and Matsuzaki S. **Suppressive effect of active hexose correlated compound (AHCC) on thymic apoptosis induced by dexamethasone in the rat.** *Endocr Regul* 34: 181-188, 2000

55. Williams DL, Sherwood ER, Browder IW, McNamee RB, Jones EL, Di Luzio NR. **Preclinical safety evaluation of soluble glucan.** Int J Immunopharmacol 1988; 10: 405-411.

56. Acute Oral Toxicity Study of NSC-24 in Rats. Essex Testing Clinic. 1990, NJ, USA.

57. Enfagro 2019. **https://www.enfagrow.com.sg/development/education-centre/wellmune-beta-glucan-enhances-body-immune-system**

58. Brousseau M, Miller SC. **Enhancement of natural killer cells and increased survival of aging mice fed daily Echinacea root extract from youth.** Biogerontology. 2005;6(3):157-63.

59. Clayton P. Ongoing research.

60. Washburn WK, Otsu I, Gottschalk R, Monaco AP: **PGG-glucan, a leukocyte-specific immunostimulant, does not potentiate GVHD or allograft rejection.** J Surg Res 62, 179-83, '96

61. Jesenak M, Banovcin P, Rennerova Z, Majtan J. **β-Glucans in the treatment and prevention of allergic diseases.** Allergol Immunopathol (Madr). 2014 Mar-Apr;42(2):149-56.

62. Talbott SM, Talbott JA, Talbott TL, Dingler E. **β-Glucan supplementation, allergy symptoms, and quality of life in self-described ragweed allergy sufferers.** Food Sci Nutr. 2013 Jan;1(1):90-101.

63. Goldman R: **Characteristics of the b-glucan receptor of murine macrophages.** Exp Cel Res 1988; 174: 481-490.

64. Moshfegh AJ, Friday JE, Goldman JP, Ahuja JKC. **Presence of Inulin and Oligofructose in the Diets of Americans.** J Nutr 129 (7), 1407S-1411S, '99.

65. Adachi K, Ohtani K, Kawano M, Singh RP, Yousuf B, Sonomoto K, Shimizu T, Nakayama J. **Metabolic dependent and independent pH-drop shuts down VirSR quorum sensing in Clostridium perfringens.** J Biosci Bioeng. 2018 May;125(5):525-531.

66. Martin-Visscher LA, Yoganathan S, Sit CS et al (2011) **The activity of bacteriocins from *Carnobacterium maltaromaticum* UAL307 against Gram-negative bacteria in combination with EDTA treatment.** FEMS Microbiol Lett 317:152–159.

67. Joseph B, Dhas B, Hena V et al (2013) **Bacteriocin from *Bacillus subtilis* as a novel drug against diabetic foot ulcer bacterial pathogens.** Asian Pac J Trop Biomed 3:942–946.

68. Starosila D, Rybalko S, Varbanetz L, Ivanskaya N, Sorokulova I. **Anti-influenza Activity of a Bacillus subtilis Probiotic Strain. Antimicrob Agents Chemother.** 2017 Jun 27;61(7).

69. Kim H, Kang SS. **Antifungal activities against Candida albicans, of cell-free supernatants obtained from probiotic Pediococcus acidilactici HW01.** Arch Oral Biol. 2019 Mar; 99:113-119.

70. Torres NI, Noll KS, Xu S, Li J, Huang Q, Sinko PJ, Wachsman MB, Chikindas ML. (2013) **Safety, formulation, and in vitro antiviral activity of the antimicrobial peptide subtilosin against herpes simplex virus type 1.** Probiotics Antimicrob Proteins 5:26–36.

71. Chen CC, Lai CC, Huang HL, Huang WY, Toh HS, Weng TC, Chuang YC, Lu YC, Tang HJ. **Antimicrobial Activity of *Lactobacillus* Species Against Carbapenem-Resistant *Enterobacteriaceae*.** Front Microbiol. 2019 Apr 18;10:789.

72. Jun JY, Jung MJ, Jeong IH, Yamazaki K, Kawai Y, Kim BM. **Antimicrobial and Antibiofilm Activities of Sulfated Polysaccharides from Marine Algae against Dental Plaque Bacteria.** Mar Drugs. 2018 Aug 27;16(9)

73. Altarac S, Papeš D. **Use of D-mannose in prophylaxis of recurrent urinary tract infections (UTIs) in women.** BJU Int. 2014 Jan;113(1):9-10.

74. Domenici L, Monti M, Bracchi C, Giorgini M, Colagiovanni V, Muzii L, Benedetti Panici P. **D-mannose: a promising support for acute urinary tract infections in women. A pilot study.** Eur Rev Med Pharmacol Sci. 2016 Jul;20(13):2920-5.

75. Babic I, Nguyen-the C, Amiot MJ, Aubert S. **Antimicrobial activity of shredded carrot extracts on food-borne bacteria and yeast.** J Appl Bacteriol. 1994 Feb;76(2):135-41.

76. Asadi A, Razavi S, Talebi M, Gholami M. **A review on anti-adhesion therapies of bacterial diseases.** Infection. 2019 Feb;47(1):13-23.

77. Neu U, Bauer J, Stehle T. **Viruses and sialic acids: rules of engagement.** Curr Opin Struct Biol. 2011 Oct;21(5):610-8.

78. Samraj AN, Bertrand KA, Luben R, Khedri Z, Yu H, Nguyen D, Gregg CJ, Diaz SL, Sawyer S, Chen X, Eliassen H, Padler-Karavani V, Wu K, Khaw KT, Willett W, Varki A. **Polyclonal**

human antibodies against glycans bearing red meat-derived non-human sialic acid N-glycolylneuraminic acid are stable, reproducible, complex and vary between individuals: Total antibody levels are associated with colorectal cancer risk. PLoS One. 2018 Jun 18;13(6):e0197464.

79. SAS study '17. Andreassen B, personal communication.
80. Abdullah, Asghar A, Butt MS, Shahid M, Huang Q. E**valuating the antimicrobial potential of green cardamom essential oil focusing on quorum sensing inhibition of *Chromobacterium violaceum*.** J Food Sci Technol. 2017 Jul;54(8):2306-2315.
81. Choo JH, Rukayadi Y, Hwang JK. **Inhibition of bacterial quorum sensing by vanilla extract. Lett Appl Microbiol.** 2006 Jun;42(6):637-41.
82. Jakobsen TH, Bragason SK, Phipps RK, Christensen LD, van Gennip M, Alhede M, Skindersoe M, Larsen TO, Høiby N, Bjarnsholt T, Givskov M. **Food as a source for quorum sensing inhibitors: iberin from horseradish revealed as a quorum sensing inhibitor of Pseudomonas aeruginosa. Appl Environ Microbiol. 2012** Apr;78(7):2410-21.
83. Krishnan T, Yin WF, Chan KG. **Inhibition of quorum sensing-controlled virulence factor production in Pseudomonas aeruginosa PAO1 by Ayurveda spice clove (Syzygium aromaticum) bud extract.** Sensors (Basel). 2012;12(4):4016-30.
84. Kumar NV, Murthy PS, Manjunatha JR, Bettadaiah BK. **Synthesis and quorum sensing inhibitory activity of key phenolic compounds of ginger and their derivatives.** Food Chem. 2014 Sep 15;159:451-7.
85. Salini R, Pandian SK. **Interference of quorum sensing in urinary pathogen Serratia marcescens by Anethum graveolens.** Pathog Dis. 2015 Aug;73(6):ftv038.
86. Cosa S, Chaudhary SK, Chen W, Combrinck S, Viljoen A. **Exploring Common Culinary Herbs and Spices as Potential Anti-Quorum Sensing Agents.** Nutrients. 2019 Mar 29;11(4). pii: E739.
87. Bjarnsholt T, Jensen PØ, Rasmussen TB, Christophersen L, Calum H, Hentzer M, Hougen HP, Rygaard J, Moser C, Eberl L, Høiby N, Givskov M.. 2005. **Garlic blocks quorum sensing and promotes rapid clearing of pulmonary Pseudomonas aeruginosa infections.** Microbiology **151**: 3873–3880
88. Hentzer M, Wu H, Andersen JB, Riedel K, Rasmussen TB, Bagge N, Kumar N, Schembri MA, Song Z, Kristoffersen P, Manefield M, Costerton JW, Molin S, Eberl L, Steinberg P, Kjelleberg S, Høiby N, Givskov M. 2003. **Attenuation of Pseudomonas aeruginosa virulence by quorum sensing inhibitors.** EMBO J. 22: 3803–3815
89. Shi L, Wu Y, Yang C, Ma Y, Zhang QZ, Huang W, Zhu XY, Yan YJ, Wang JX, Zhu T, Qu D, Zheng CQ, Zhao KQ. **Effect of nicotine on Staphylococcus aureus biofilm formation and virulence factors. Sci Rep.** 2019 Dec 27;9(1):20243.
90. Wu Y, Ma Y, Xu T, Zhang QZ, Bai J, Wang J, Zhu T, Lou Q, Götz F, Qu D, Zheng CQ, Zhao KQ. **Nicotine Enhances *Staphylococcus epidermidis* Biofilm Formation by Altering the Bacterial Autolysis, Extracellular DNA Releasing, and Polysaccharide Intercellular Adhesin Production. Front Microbiol.** 2018 Oct 29;9:2575.
91. Holick MF, Chen TC. **Vitamin D deficiency: A worldwide problem with health consequences.** Am J Clin Nutr. 2008;87:1080S–6S.
92. Beck M. A, Shi Q, Morris VG, Levander OA. (1995) R**apid genomic evolution of a non-virulent coxsackievirus B3 in selenium-deficient mice results in selection of identical virulent isolates.** *Nat. Med.* **1**,433-436
93. Beck MA, Levander OA, Handy J (2003) **Selenium Deficiency and Viral Infection.** J Nutr 133(5):1463S-1467S
94. Rayman, M. (1997) **Dietary selenium: time to act.** *British Medical Journal*, **314**, 387- 8.
95. Vinceti M, Filippini T, Cilloni S, Crespi CM. **The Epidemiology of Selenium and Human Cancer. Adv Cancer** Res. 2017;136:1-48

96. **https://www.immunology.org/sites/default/files/connect-immune-research-are-you-autoimmune-report.pdf**

97. Manzel A, Muller DN, Hafler DA, Erdman SE, Linker RA, Kleinewietfeld M. **Role of "Western diet" in inflammatory autoimmune diseases.** Curr Allergy Asthma Rep. 2014 Jan;14(1):404.

98. Ahmad S, Mu X, Yang F, Greenwald E, Park JW, Jacob E, Zhang CZ, Hur S. **Breaching Self-Tolerance to Alu Duplex RNA Underlies MDA5-Mediated Inflammation.** Cell. 2018 Feb 8;172(4):797-810.e13.

99. Kusalik A, Bickis M, Lewis C, Li Y, Lucchese G, Marincola FM, Kanduc D. **Widespread and ample peptide overlapping between HCV and Homo sapiens proteomes.** Peptides. 2007 Jun;28(6):1260-7.

100. Kowarsky M, Camunas-Soler J, Kertesz M, De Vlaminck I, Koh W, Pan W, Martin L, Neff NF, Okamoto J, Wong RJ, Kharbanda S, El-Sayed Y, Blumenfeld Y, Stevenson DK, Shaw GM, Wolfe ND, Quake SR. **Numerous uncharacterized and highly divergent microbes which colonize humans are revealed by circulating cell-free DNA.** Proc Natl Acad Sci U S A. 2017 Sep 5;114(36):9623-9628.

101. Ogrendik M. **Antibiotics for the treatment of rheumatoid arthritis.** Int J Gen Med. 2013 Dec 27;7:43-7.

102. Manfredo Vieira S, Hiltensperger M, Kumar V, Zegarra-Ruiz D, Dehner C, Khan N, Costa FRC, Tiniakou E, Greiling T, Ruff W, Barbieri A, Kriegel C, Mehta SS, Knight JR, Jain D, Goodman AL, Kriegel MA. **Translocation of a gut pathobiont drives autoimmunity in mice and humans.** Science. 2018 Mar 9;359(6380):1156-1161.

103. Sultan AA, Mallen C, Muller S, Hider S, Scott I, Helliwell T, Hall LJ. **Antibiotic use and the risk of rheumatoid arthritis: a population-based case-control study.** BMC Med. 2019; 17: 154.

104. Jobin K, Stumpf NE, Schwab S, Eichler M, Neubert P, Rauh M, Adamowski M, Babyak O, Hinze D, Sivalingam S, Weisheit C, Hochheiser K, Schmidt S, Meissner M, Garbi N, Abdullah Z, Wenzel U, Hölzel M, Jantsch J, Kurts C. **A high-salt diet compromises antibacterial neutrophil responses through hormonal perturbation.** *Science Translational Medicine* 25 Mar 2020:Vol. 12, Issue 536, eaay3850

105. Czop JK, Austen KF '85: **A b-glucan inhibitable receptor on human monocytes: its identity with the phagocytic receptor for particulate activators of the alternative complement pathway.** J Immunol 1985; 134: 2588-2593.

106. Onderdonk AB, Cisneros RL, Hinkson P, Ostroff G: **Anti-infective effect of poly-beta-1,6-glucotriosyl-beta 1,3glucapyranose glucan in vivo.** Infection & Immunity 60:1642-1647, '92

107. Vetvicka V, Terayama K, Mandeville R, Brousseau P, Kournikakis B, Ostroff G: **Pilot Study: Orally-Administered Yeast Beta1,3-glucan Prophylactically Protects Against Anthrax Infection and Cancer in Mice;** J Am Nutraceutical Assocn 5:1-5, '02

108. Kernodle DS, Gates H, Kaiser AB: **Prophylactic Anti-Infective Activity of Poly-(1-6)-beta-D—Glucapyranosyl-(1-3)-beta-D-Glucapyranose Glucan in a Guinea Pig Model of Staphylococcal Wound Infection.** Antimicrob Agents & Chemother 42:545-549, '98

109. W.H.O. 2013. **https://www.who.int/influenza_vaccines_plan/resources/session_10_kaddar.pdf**

110. Courthouse News 2010: **https://www.courthousenews.com/Class-Says-Merck-Lied-About-Mumps-Vaccine/**

111. CDC 2019. **https://www.cdc.gov/flu/prevent/guillainbarre.htm**

112. https://www.covid.is/data

113. Coussens AK, Martineau AR, Wilkinson RJ. **Anti-Inflammatory and Antimicrobial Actions of Vitamin D in Combating TB/HIV.** Scientifica (Cairo). 2014;2014:903680.

114. Tsuji PA, Carlson BA, Anderson CB, Seifried HE, Hatfield DL, Howard MT. **Dietary Selenium Levels Affect Selenoprotein Expression and Support the Interferon-γ and IL-6 Immune Response Pathways in Mice.** Nutrients. 2015 Aug 6;7(8):6529-49.

115. te Velthuis AJ, van den Worm SH, Sims AC, Baric RS, Snijder EJ, van Hemert MJ. **Zn(2+) inhibits coronavirus and arterivirus RNA polymerase activity in vitro and zinc ionophores block the replication of these viruses in cell culture.** PLoS Pathog. 2010 Nov 4;6(11):e1001176.

116. Patel U, Gingerich A, Widman L, Sarr D, Tripp RA, Rada B. **Susceptibility of influenza virus to hypothiocyanite and hypoiodite produced by lactoperoxidase in a cell-free system.** PLoS One. 2018 Jul 25;13(7):e0199167.

117. Gingerich A, Pang L, Hanson J, Dlugolenski D, Streich R, Lafontaine ER, Nagy T, Tripp RA, Rada B. **Hypothiocyanite produced by human and rat respiratory epithelial cells inactivates extracellular H1N2 influenza A virus.** Inflamm Res. 2016; 65(1):71–80.

118. Cegolon L, Salata C, Piccoli E, Juarez V, Palu G, Mastrangelo G, Calistri A. **In vitro antiviral activity of hypothiocyanite against A/H1N1/2009 pandemic influenza virus.** Int J Hyg Environ Health. 2014; 217(1):17–22.

119. Sugita C, Shin K, Wakabayashi H, Tsuhako R, Yoshida H, Watanabe W, Kurokawa M. **Antiviral activity of hypothiocyanite produced by lactoperoxidase against influenza A and B viruses and mode of its antiviral action.** Acta Virol. 2018;62(4):401-408.

120. Panon G, Tache S, Labie C. **Antiviral Substances in Raw Bovine Milk Active Against Bovine Rotavirus and Coronavirus.** J Food Protection. 1987: 50:862-886

121. Fischer, JA. **Augmenting antiviral host defense in the respiratory epithelium.** PhD thesis, University of Iowa, 2009. https://doi.org/10.17077/etd.9hpirtqh

122. Xiang D, Sharma VR, Freter CE, Yan J. **Anti tumor monoclonal antibodies in conjunction with β-glucans: a novel anti-cancer immunotherapy. Curr Med Chem.** 2012;19(25):4298-305.

123. Kampf G, Todt D, Pfaender S, Steinmann E. **Persistence of coronaviruses on inanimate surfaces and their inactivation with biocidal agents. Journal of Hospital Infection Volume 104, Issue 3,** March 2020, Pages 246-251

Made in the USA
San Bernardino, CA
28 April 2020